daily affirmation

I am Powerful, Positive, Productive,
Peaceful, Purposeful, Prayerful and Profitable.
I am chosen by God, loved by God and protected by God.
I am loved, lovable, strong, faithful, unique, creative. I will lead and not follow; I am the head and not the tail.
I am the lender not the borrower.
I am above, not beneath.
I am a force of good defying the odds. I have a lot of blessings coming to me. No weapon formed against me shall prosper. Every tongue that rises up against me in judgement shall be condemned. I am excitedly joyful.
God will lead and send people to me to bless me.
God will lead and send me to people to bless.
I am humbly healthy wealthy a winner.
I will live the fulfilling life God has for me.
I believe it, I see it, I feel it, I receive it,
Great things are coming to me!.

My short term goals for the next 1-2 years are...

My long term goals for the next 3-5 years are...

I pray for and I pray that...

I am grateful for...

Fear not, for I am with you; be not dismay, for I am your God; I will strengthen you, I will help you, I will uphold you with my righteous right hand.

- Isaiah 41:10

For God has not given us the spirit of fear but of power and of love and a sound mind.

- 2 Timothy 1:7

Trust in the lord with all your heart and lean not to your own understanding; in all your ways acknowledge/submit to Him, and He will make your paths straight.

- Proverbs 3:5-6

Create in me a clean heart,
O God; and renew a right
spirit within me.

- Psalm 51:10

The Lord is my shepherd I shall not want. He maketh me to lie down in green pastures: He leadeth me beside the still waters. He restoreth my soul: he leadeth me in the paths of righteousness for his name's sake.

- Psalm 23: 1-3

Joshua 1:9

Be strong and courageous

Psalm 34:4-5

I sought the Lord, and he heard me,
and delivered me from all my fears.

Ecclesiastes 9:11

The race is not given to the swift nor to the strong

Psalm 46:10

Be still and know that I am God.

Phil 4:13

I can do all things through Christ which strengthens me

Change your ending and story in a positive way

Know that you are beautiful and wonderfully made

Trust your God mind,
because it is God

Place your faith over your fears

Proudly loving ME!

Always Grateful and Thankful

Expect a Blessing!

Think on good things

Positive, productive, peaceful and prayerful

Renew your mind daily

Demand the best from yourself and nothing less.

www.ingramcontent.com/pod-product-compliance
Ingram Content Group UK Ltd.
Pitfield, Milton Keynes, MK11 3LW, UK
UKHW021836270726
14058UKWH00002B/186

9 781458 309174